IMAGES
of America

TACOMA'S POINT DEFIANCE PARK

Park Superintendent Ebenezer Roberts (first row, far right) and others take a break from their daily labor to pose for a picture. The occasion for this photograph is unknown, but with gardening tools in the foreground and samples of plants in the workers' hands, it may have been intended to highlight the planting and cleanup underway in the park. (Courtesy Jean Insel Robeson.)

On the Cover: On July 4, 1924, the finalists in the Tacoma Yacht Club's Bathing Girl Review pose for the camera near the Point Defiance Park Boathouse Pavilion. Grace Copeland (far right) was chosen Tacoma's most beautiful bathing beauty in her light blue woolen bathing costume. Her court of 10 was selected from a total of 32 contestants. (Courtesy TPL.)

IMAGES
of America

TACOMA'S POINT DEFIANCE PARK

Melissa McGinnis, Doreen Beard-Simpkins, and
the Metropolitan Park District of Tacoma

ARCADIA
PUBLISHING

ISBN 978-0-7385-9591-7

Published by Arcadia Publishing
Charleston, South Carolina

Printed in the United States of America

Library of Congress Control Number: 2012937311

For all general information, please contact Arcadia Publishing:
Telephone 843-853-2070
Fax 843-853-0044
E-mail sales@arcadiapublishing.com
For customer service and orders:
Toll-Free 1-888-313-2665

Visit us on the Internet at www.arcadiapublishing.com

Every citizen of Tacoma should feel it a duty and privilege to become one of the guardians.

—Hare & Hare Point Defiance Park Plan, 1911

Contents

Acknowledgments

Theirs were the sweat, pick and shovel calluses, and frustrations. Theirs was the long vision of the future which transformed Point Defiance from a wilderness into a beautiful park.

—Trillium Roberts Insel, as quoted in the *Tacoma News Tribune*, March 5, 1967.

We could not have said it better. Our primary acknowledgment is to all of those—past, present, and future—whose steady, unsung labor in weather both fair and foul makes Point Defiance Park so spectacular.

Along with those who plant, nurture, trim, build, and conserve, the authors applaud our fellow Tacomans who serve as stewards of this impressive piece of civic real estate. As the decades pass since the federal government transferred its title to the city's full municipal ownership in the early 20th century, past and present citizens of Tacoma have upheld the responsibility entrusted to them by Pres. Theodore Roosevelt in 1905. Our mutual reward for this long and dedicated stewardship is a city park as magnificent as Point Defiance.

Among these civic stewards, we acknowledge the leadership of the present Board of Park Commissioners: Larry Dahl, Erik Hanberg, Aaron Pointer, Tim Reid, Andrea Smith, and Executive Director Jack C. Wilson. For collegial assistance on this project, Metro Parks Tacoma (MPT) communications coordinator Sheree Trefry earns our special thanks for doing another star turn as the technician preparing the historic images for publication. We also recognize and thank MPT researcher Bill Rhind for his co-authorship of the *1905–2005 Point Defiance Park Centennial History*, which supports the narrative of the present book, and research assistant Samantha Litwin for her tireless transcription of 44 years of handwritten park board minutes.

The ever-professional staff of the Northwest Room of the Tacoma Public Library, and the collections they manage and research, are a tremendous credit to the library system of the city of Tacoma. Thank you Brian Kamens, Bob Schuler, and Jeanie Fisher for your scholarship.

Finally, to Francis and to Ebenezer, our heartfelt appreciation for resolutions and roses.

All images without a credit are the property of Metro Parks Tacoma. Full image credit information is provided on page 127.

INTRODUCTION

Tacoma's Great Pride. Such was the headline description of Point Defiance Park in the feature article of the *Tacoma Daily Ledger* of July 3, 1892, barely four years after the city had started basic improvements on the park's rugged tract of forest and steep waterfront in 1888. The peninsula was then a considerable distance from the little burg of Tacoma that at the time just hugged the hillsides above Pacific Avenue and Old Town. In fact, not until 1905 would the young city even hold the deed to the park of which it was already so proud.

The natural history of Point Defiance Park goes back millennia. Bordered on three sides by the tidal waters of Puget Sound, the peninsula was carved by glaciers, wave action, and earthquakes over tens of thousands of years. Once formed by eons of such geological forces, over time the flora and fauna of Point Defiance developed into a native forest with plant and animal biodiversity characteristic of the Lowland Puget Sound region. The native peoples who inhabited this area for centuries before the late 18th-century arrival of Europeans and Americans also contributed explanations and names for the peninsula's interesting terrain. In Whulshootseed, the language of the Southern Puget Sound Salish people, the name for Point Defiance was pronounced *s-cheet-oos*, which linguists translate as "near face" or "near cliff" and interpret as a reference to the proximity of Point Defiance to the land across the Narrows. The name *jeeq-shud*, meaning "wet feet," referred to the incurved shore of the west side, while *cho-cho-thlap*, which translated as "vine maples," denoted the site of a good clam-digging beach on the southeast shore. Native peoples used the peninsula as an itinerant campsite, but there is no record of any permanent indigenous settlement.

The name "Point Defiance"—often a curiosity to Tacoma visitors and newcomers—came into existence in the mid-19th century courtesy of an officer of the United States Navy. The United States Exploring Expedition (1838–1842), popularly referred to as the Wilkes Expedition after its US Navy commander, Charles Wilkes, spent the summer of 1841 in this region—long before the city of Tacoma or the state of Washington even existed—creating maps and charts. The name "Point Defiance" appears on Charles Wilkes's 1841 map of Puget Sound, which seems to be its first recorded use. A few years later, Wilkes's 1849 personal account of the expedition describes the strategic military potential of the peninsular geography for the young and westward-moving United States, stating that "the Narrows, if strongly fortified, would bid defiance to any attack." So, Point Defiance it became.

Once named in recognition of the peninsula's strategic location, Point Defiance sparked the interest of the US government, and in 1866, Pres. Andrew Johnson set aside the approximately 640 acres of Point Defiance by executive order as a federal military reservation. In the latter half of the 19th century, the United States set aside many such prominent Puget Sound locations for possible future use as lighthouse or fortification sites. The result was that, as the young city of Tacoma established itself and aimed for prosperity and growth from the 1860s through the 1880s, the Point Defiance acreage was off-limits to development due to its federal reservation status. Its considerable distance from the city, combined with the lack of road improvements and land transportation, also precluded much interest in the heavily wooded peninsula, other than the odd adventurer arriving by water to camp on its beaches or the occasional opportunist cutting firewood.

All that changed in 1888. By then, the canny real estate developers of Tacoma's western edge proposed a plan for a streetcar line to link new neighborhoods to the jobs and commerce centered on downtown Pacific Avenue. They recognized that a prominent park at the end of the planned residential development would entice home buyers. With a streetcar going all the way "out to the Point," a park might even be an attractive destination in its own right. But first, the permission of the federal government had to be obtained, since it held the title to the potential park land. Tacoma's prominent businessmen and civic boosters turned their persuasive powers to courting Washington, DC, for the go-ahead. Many of them had considerable financial interests in the real estate and transportation companies that would benefit, though that was not a problem back in the proverbial day. At the end of 1888, Pres. Grover Cleveland signed the legislation that permitted Tacoma to develop the Point Defiance military reservation acreage into a city park, with a clause preserving the federal right to take it back at any time should the need arise. Little more than a year later, in 1890, the Point Defiance–Tacoma–Edison Railway Company celebrated completion of the streetcar line to the wilds of Point Defiance Park, and the city created its first Board of Park Commissioners to govern its fledgling park system (the only others at the time were Ferry Park, Puget Park, and Wright Park).

Tacoma's "great pride" in these accomplishments was part of a larger, national American trend in park planning during the second half of the 19th century. The ultimate goal of designing landscapes for public use and enjoyment was the improvement of American society through harmonious public spaces that were to serve as an antidote to the increasing urbanization of post–Civil War America. Parks were to be graceful, democratic, and rejuvenating, separate from the intrusions of daily life, and sheltered as much as possible from conflicting uses. The design philosophy's best-known proponent was the renowned landscape architect Frederick Law Olmsted (1822–1903), and though neither he nor the firm he established designed any of Tacoma's public parks, this spirit of artful rejuvenation in the design of civic green space was very present as Point Defiance evolved from peninsula to park. The pages that follow trace a fond journey, from the decades leading to Tacoma's 1905 title to Point Defiance Park, through the city's sustained investment of several generations over the past century.

Proud of Point Defiance Park?

Yes, indeed.

One

"Tacoma's Sound Shore Retreat"

"To make a big park in a new city is slow work" declared the *Tacoma Daily Ledger* on June 3, 1900, referring to the previous 12 years.

Once the federal government granted Tacoma the right to develop the Point Defiance military reservation as a park in 1888, the young city lost no time in taking the first steps to make the peninsula its own. In 1890, it appointed a Board of Park Commissioners to serve the city council in an advisory capacity. Their first order of business that same year was to hire a visionary landscape architect, Edward Otto Schwagerl (1842–1910), who thought on a grand scale. "Parks are full of Nature's innocent and holy inspirations, and in them are whispers of peace and joy," he said. "Parks are the breathing lungs and beating hearts of great cities." But Schwagerl stayed in Tacoma for only two years before leaving to design Seattle parks. In the same year, the board also hired Ebenezer Rhys Roberts (1854–1918), a no-nonsense gardener who got his hands dirty immediately by planting all of Tacoma's early parks, and who actually lived in Point Defiance Park to guard its flora and fauna, laboring on the slow work of creating a park. His hand is still visible today.

Point Defiance Park in the 1890s was a diamond in the rough. Roberts's workaday challenges included grading the entry bowl area by horse, wheelbarrow, and the occasional stick of dynamite, as well as figuring out how to plant and maintain hardscrabble flower beds and rose cuttings with no reservoir of fresh water. A political challenge—thankfully abandoned—was a proposition in 1899 to relocate the state penitentiary from McNeil Island to the park's west side.

By 1900, the 10 years of toil "to make a big park in a new city" at last had resulted in a sylvan destination perched on the shore that rapidly became Tacoma's favorite day trip and "Sound shore retreat."

Charles Wilkes (1798–1877) led the United States Exploring Expedition, which circumnavigated the globe and spent the summer of 1841 charting Puget Sound waters. The name "Point Defiance" appears on his 1841 map of Puget Sound, which seems to be the first recorded use of the name.

Francis W. Cushman (1867–1909) was the US representative for the congressional district that included Tacoma from 1899 to his untimely death in 1909. House Resolution 17019 was his pet project to transfer ownership of Point Defiance Park from the federal government to Tacoma. Pres. Theodore Roosevelt signed the legislation on March 3, 1905.

Allen C. Mason (1855–1920) was one of Tacoma's leading civic boosters of the 1880s, with handsome real estate investments. When the federal government granted Tacoma the right to develop Point Defiance as a park in 1888, Mason occasionally advanced his own money for construction of the streetcar line out "to the Point." He drove the final stake himself at its March 1, 1890, dedication.

Bernice Newell was a local newspaper reporter. When Pres. Theodore Roosevelt visited Tacoma in May 1903, she penned a very popular sentiment in the May 23, 1903, *Tacoma Daily Ledger*: "Mr. President, don't you think it would be only fair if Uncle Sam would fix it so Tacoma could have Point Defiance Park for her very own?"

Edward Otto Schwagerl (1842–1910), Bavarian by birth, grew up in Paris and New York City. His European and American educations gave him an appreciation for the confluence of art, architecture, nature, and landscape design. Schwagerl worked in Tacoma from 1890 to 1892 on the initial plans for both Wright Park and Point Defiance Park.

A native of Wales, Ebenezer Rhys Roberts (1854–1918) arrived in Tacoma in 1888 and worked on private estates until he was hired by the Board of Park Commissioners to implement Schwagerl's vision of Wright Park. When Schwagerl left to design Seattle parks in 1892, Roberts took over as visionary, green thumb, and eventually superintendent for all of Tacoma's early parks. (Courtesy Jean Insel Robeson, granddaughter of Ebenezer Roberts.)

Transportation from Tacoma out to Point Defiance Park in the era before roads were developed or private cars were common was either by boat or by streetcar. In the 1890s, the "[street]car station" in Point Defiance Park consisted of this simple rustic shelter situated where the Pagoda building stands today. (Courtesy Jean Insel Robeson.)

In contrast to what appear to be park visitors dressed for summer in the top photograph, these passengers on the Point Defiance–Tacoma–Edison Railway are clad more for the inclement weather of the off-season. Edison was the name of the area in the vicinity of present-day South Tacoma Way and South Fifty-sixth Street. (Courtesy TPL.)

A short-lived but memorable Point Defiance pastime of the 1890s was the informal creation of summer campsites for extended stays on the park's shores. In this photograph, the residents of "Camp HooHoo" in the summer of 1894 clearly enjoyed the pleasures of an idyllic spot. In 1896, the Board of Park Commissioners charged $3 per site for the season. Summer campers had the bounty of the beach as well as the limited waterfront amenities of the time, such as rustic fruit stands set up by enterprising concessionaires. These conveniences would grow in sophistication over the next decade, catering to the growing number of park visitors and making the destination ever more popular. (Courtesy WSHS.)

Hired by the Board of Park Commissioners in 1890 for the clearing and planting work underway in Point Defiance Park, Ebenezer Rhys Roberts was a Welshman with a young family in tow. Shown at one of Roberts's rustic park benches in this c. 1900 photograph are, from left to right, Ebenezer, his wife Mary Ann, infant daughter Trillium, daughter Reseda, and son Ebenezer Jr. (Courtesy Jean Insel Robeson.)

Another Roberts family photograph captures Reseda (left) and Trillium with the youngest Roberts son, Woodland, affectionately known as "Woody," on a day in Point Defiance Park around 1907. They are seated on another rustic bench built by their father, which is positioned on the deck of the waterfront pavilion, built in 1903. (Courtesy Jean Insel Robeson.)

The three youngest Roberts children, from left to right, Woodland, Reseda, and Trillium, are pictured around 1907 on the lawn of the Lodge, built in 1898 as the Roberts home in the park. The eldest child, Ebenezer Jr., is not pictured. As an elderly woman, Trillium wrote detailed reminiscences of living in Point Defiance in her childhood. (Courtesy Jean Insel Robeson.)

A wonderful family photograph of Ebenezer Roberts shows the consummate gardener in tweed vest and trousers, replete with flowers in the band of his hat. Roberts was such a devoted horticulturist that he gave three of his four children botanical names—Reseda, Trillium, and Woodland. (Courtesy Jean Insel Robeson.)

One of the earliest improvements in Point Defiance Park was the construction of a log bridge in 1892 designed by park board secretary F.I. Mead. This bridge, seen at right, was the gateway from the developed areas located closer to the entrance of the park to the wild, forested areas toward the point. It bridged a gulch, and a stream underneath was dammed to create a pond, which in turn was crossed by a series of smaller picturesque rustic bridges, as shown below. The Rustic Bridge, made of some 3,500 logs, was 250 feet in length and 80 feet high. Though replaced by fill and a paved roadbed in 1933–1934, the locale today is recalled by the aptly named Rustic Picnic Area.

The roadbed level of the Rustic Bridge afforded spectacular views overlooking Puget Sound to the west and into the deep woods to the east. The road itself was turf, and wood plank sidewalks flanked each side. The bridge was a very popular subject of postcards at the turn of the 20th century; this one was postmarked July 5, 1904.

A closer view of the same side and section of the Rustic Bridge features gardener and park superintendent Ebenezer Roberts with a steadying hand safely on his daughter Trillium, perched on the edge of the rail overlooking the gulch and picturesque streams and smaller bridges below. Trillium's hat is at his feet. (Courtesy Jean Insel Robeson.)

The Board of Park Commissioners approved $2,220 to build a residence in Point Defiance Park in 1898 for Superintendent Ebenezer Roberts, originally referred to as the Keeper's Lodge. It was designed by noted Tacoma architect C.A. Darmer. Roberts and his family were permitted to live in the park, where he could more easily supervise the crews clearing and grading the paths and roads, tend the emerging gardens, feed the zoo animals, and provide general park security. These early construction photographs show an open view of the side and the front elevation of the house that, at the time, would have had a view of Puget Sound. Today, this same prospect of the Lodge is obscured by trees and gardens. (Courtesy C.A. Darmer, grandson of the original architect.)

An early newspaper description of the Lodge referred to it as "an ideal rural home, built of polished peeled logs, with an immense colonial verandah running around the entire house." This c. 1900 photograph shows the kitchen door side entrance of the Lodge shortly after its completion, with one of the Point Defiance zoo peacocks sitting on the gate. (Courtesy TPL.)

By 1920, the Lodge was established among the maturing landscape of Point Defiance Park. Ebenezer Roberts left the employ of the park in 1908, so the Lodge was likely home to Superintendent George Hill at this time. Hill served from 1910 to 1921. This photograph shows the structure from the same angle as the 1898 construction photographs on the previous page. (Courtesy of UW.)

The Lodge, pictured above from the front in 1982, served as the home of Tacoma's park superintendents and executive directors from 1898, when the Ebenezer Roberts family moved into the brand new house, to 1980, when the William Glundberg family moved out. Other superintendents who combined residence in Point Defiance Park with administration duties for the entire Metropolitan Park District included Floyd and Agnes Owen, pictured below at the Lodge when it was their home. Floyd Owen was a 47-year employee for whom the park's Owen Beach is named. From 1980 to 2012, the Lodge served as a gracious wedding, party, and meeting facility. Today, it has a new role as a summer season Visitor Center with information on park history, ecology, destinations, and events. (Courtesy Floyd Owen family.)

Another structure in the park's early years was the original Job Carr cabin, "the birthplace of Tacoma." Clinton P. Ferry was a Tacoma businessman who had donated property to the City of Tacoma in 1883 for its first park. In 1899, Ferry turned his attention to Point Defiance, spearheading the effort to relocate the Carr cabin from its original Old Town site to the park. In 1900, the cabin was moved to a location adjacent to the park's streetcar tracks near the present tennis courts, on the bluff above the Vashon Island–Point Defiance ferry landing, as shown above. In 1917, the Job Carr cabin moved once more, to the entrance of Five Mile Drive (shown below), where it resided for decades before deteriorating in the forest's marine climate. Ultimately it was dismantled and removed from Point Defiance; a reproduction now stands in Old Town Park.

In 1901, a major feature appeared in the Point Defiance Park entry area—its first greenhouse. Situated between the Keeper's Lodge and the location of today's Rose Garden, the structure's original footprint measured 25 by 100 feet and cost $2,000 to build. An additional wing later expanded the square footage for the requirements of serving as both a production greenhouse for plant propagation and as a conservatory for exotic plants and palms. The photograph below shows the scope of the structure that sheltered the seedlings and rootstock tended by the park's crew of gardeners. The attached wooden structure on the right served as a tool and supplies storage shed.

In this c. 1906 photograph, Ebenezer Roberts is shown at work on a floral array in the Point Defiance greenhouse, just steps from his home in the Lodge. Even though the structure was only five years old at the time, its propagation and public display functions were already at odds, as a steady stream of visitors inhibited Roberts's horticultural work. (Courtesy Jean Insel Robeson.)

Park visitors, such as the Lars Larson family, shown here in a c. 1903 photograph, flocked to the park's greenhouse to see exotic banana trees, royal palms, and other imported species. By the early 1920s, the Point Defiance greenhouse production functions were removed to newer structures in the southeastern acreage of the park, and the commanding edifice was dismantled. (Courtesy Dorothy Thortyacre.)

Another early Point Defiance Park amenity that attracted visitors in droves was a Concert Garden, further refined with a band shell in 1901. This area was located on the far side of today's Pagoda, where the lawn sweeps down to meet the edge of the bluff overlooking the boathouse. In those days, the view included an open expanse of Puget Sound.

This view of the Concert Garden, also known as the Music Court, includes the rows of the park's rustic benches awaiting the next audience. Sunday band concerts became a regular feature of summer months in Point Defiance Park; refreshment stands stood close by for lemonade or a bag of peanuts during intermissions. The Music Court reverted to open lawn with the construction of the Pagoda in 1914. (Courtesy WSHS.)

The Pearl Street entrance to Point Defiance Park was framed by a giant log arch designed and built in 1906 by Superintendent Ebenezer Rhys Roberts, visible toward the right in this photograph taken from inside the park. This impressive entry was known as the Cushman Arch, in honor of US Congressional representative Francis W. Cushman, who had helped transfer the park's title to Tacoma in 1905.

While of impressive stature, the 1906 Cushman Arch at the park entrance was short-lived; for unknown reasons, it was gone from Point Defiance by 1911. After Francis Cushman's untimely death in 1909, his family commissioned this memorial statue, dedicated in 1925, which still stands near the main Point Defiance Park entrance.

In the early years of Point Defiance Park, postcards and newspapers alike referred to "spooning" in Tacoma's parks as a popular pastime. This archaic term from a century ago referred to couples being openly sentimental with one another; a present-day term might be *PDA* (public display of affection). While the newspaper articles tended to frown slightly on the practice, the postcards of the day appeared to celebrate the many prime park locations for spooning, with photographic titles such as "Lovers Retreat" and "Lovers Lane." The latter was the name for the area below the Rustic Bridge, where picturesque ponds, leafy glades, and rustic benches beckoned those with an appreciation for all of nature's beauty.

The many paths traversing the bluffs down to the Point Defiance shore in the early years also featured rustic byways where the young and the young-at-heart could appreciate the park's scenery. At left, a young man nattily dressed in knickers and argyle socks appears oblivious to the postcard photographer. Instead, he seems entirely concentrated on his female companion, whose summer hat is visible just beside his cap. The postcard below dates to around 1905, as defined by the "Watch Tacoma Grow" slogan flying on the pennant from the top of the 1903 waterfront pavilion. Tacoma boosters adopted it as the city's official slogan, and it became nationally known. More than a century later, the slogan is still proudly used in an affectionate "retro" sense.

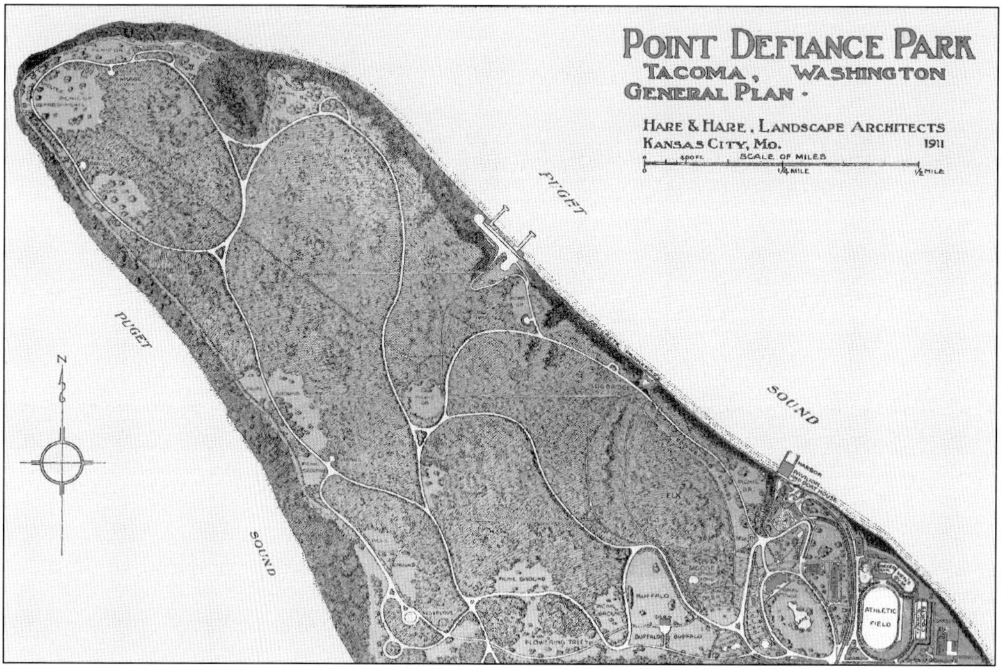

In 1910, the Board of Park Commissioners engaged the services of Hare & Hare, a prominent Kansas City, Missouri, landscape architectural firm, to create the first formal plan for Point Defiance Park. The firm's team spent two weeks in March 1911 hiking the park's rugged acreage and taking measurements and photographs. This map was part of the full plan the firm presented to the park board in July 1911.

In the same summer of 1911, a young girl extolled the existing beauty of Point Defiance on the back of a park postcard. The Hare & Hare Plan of 1911 was intended to augment that perception, but it also signaled a change in direction from the early Ebenezer Roberts years, toward a more formalized and intentional process of park design.

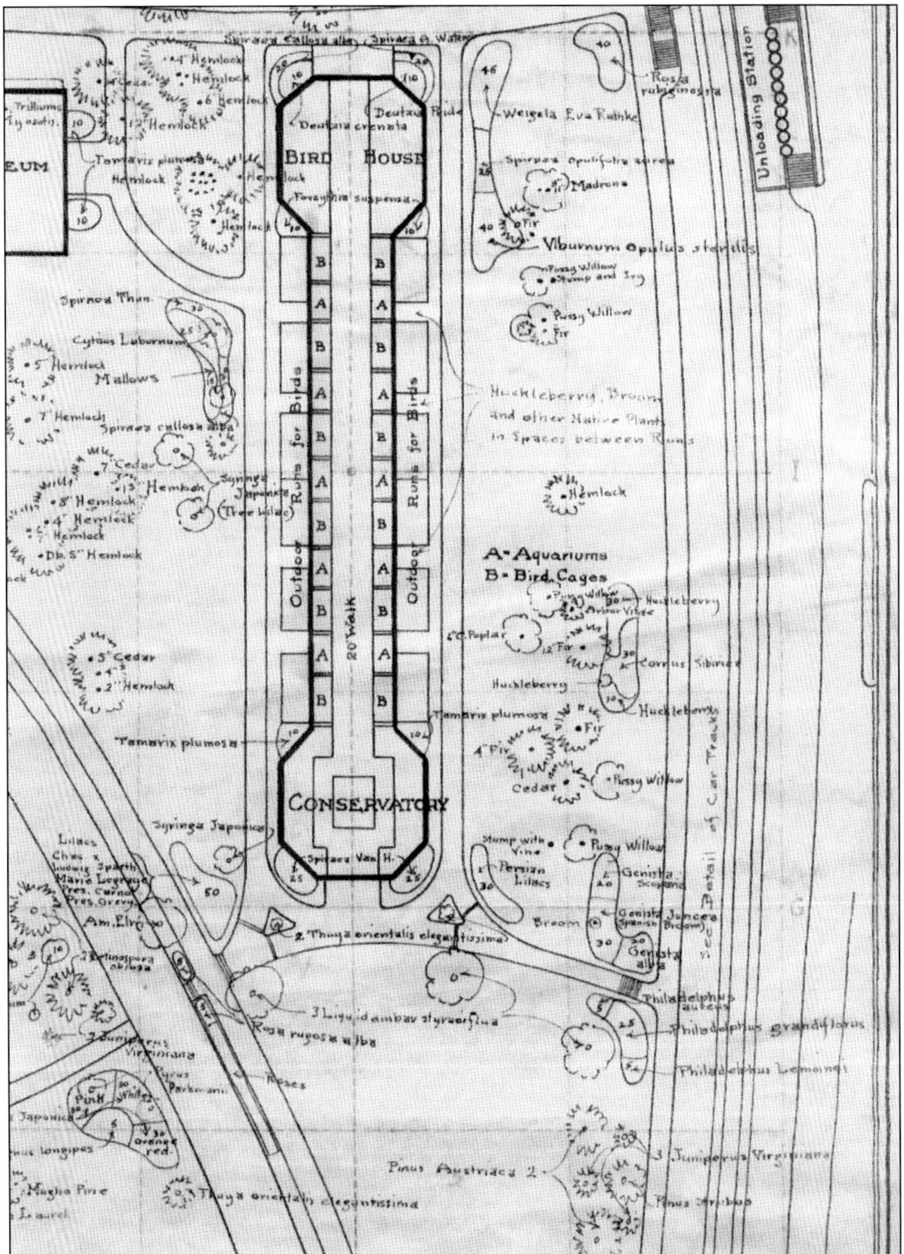

The Hare & Hare Plan of 1911 was impressive in its scope and its detail of proposed designs for planting, improvements of general amenities, and the addition of entirely new structures. One section of the plan, shown here, includes the Point Defiance Park drive in the lower left corner, just inside the main Pearl Street entrance. To the right of the drive, situated on what is now the open lawn hilltop, Hare & Hare proposed construction of "a low glass house . . . a combined aviary, aquarium, and fern house . . . [and to] design the whole building in conformity to the Japanese architecture." Another suggested structure, in the upper left corner, was to be a "Zoological Museum" with mounted and fossil specimens of extant and extinct species. The Hare & Hare plan was never realized, except for one major structure. (Courtesy TPL.)

This Hare & Hare drawing details the firm's plan for the garden proposed for the foot of the new streetcar station, but it is their suggestion for the Japanese architecture of the new station itself that commands attention. The rustic shelter that had sufficed as a passenger shelter in the Ebenezer Roberts era was to make way in 1914 for the beloved structure known today as the Pagoda.

An early postcard view of the Pagoda shows the new streetcar station not fully finished. The angle of this photograph is from an oblique point of view to the above drawing. The new station awaits its iconic tile roof, and the Japanese garden is yet to be planted, but this view remains recognizable almost a century later.

Two c. 1915 photographs of the Pagoda from the side of the streetcar track reveal views very similar to today, except for the mode of transportation. The tracks made a teardrop-shaped loop at the station, where passengers alighted for a day in the park or climbed back on to find seats for the return trip to Tacoma. From the Pagoda, paths led park visitors down to the pleasures of the waterfront, or across the road to stroll the gardens or visit the zoological collection, whose pens in those days extended down into the gardens areas. (Below image courtesy Tom Stenger.)

The interior of the new 1914 Pagoda featured amenities not available in the previous rustic shelter that served as the streetcar station. Built in an eclectic Japanese temple style, as advocated by the 1911 Hare & Hare Plan, and initially referred to simply as "the Car Station," the Pagoda served as a waiting room for streetcar passengers, and also featured restrooms—or "comfort stations" in the parlance of the day—and first aid facilities on the lower level. Additional luxuries included rocking chairs and, in the summer season, an attendant to hand out towels in the ladies' restroom. Men visiting the Pagoda enjoyed a separate smoking room and marble lavatories. One end of the building boasted the fireplace still in existence today, while the other featured a retail counter with at least one pair of tennis racquets.

Architect Luther Twichell designed the 1914 Pagoda in the general Japanese style favored by the Hare & Hare Plan of 1911, but their intention that the structure be surrounded by Japanese-influenced garden design took decades to realize. This photograph shows the new Pagoda with a very basic and generic planting bed on the streetcar-turnaround side. (Courtesy TPL.)

This view of the downhill side of the Pagoda shows the streetcar station around 1930, still with very traditional lawn and tree landscaping. In 1963, a two-year project sponsored by the Capitol District of Garden Clubs finally began to give this side of the Pagoda more of the Japanese ambience familiar to present-day park visitors. (Courtesy Christine Dennett.)

In 1938, the City of Tacoma changed its principal system of public transportation from streetcar to bus, so the Pagoda followed suit, serving Point Defiance for a time as the bus terminus. However, as the park's zoo and waterfront regions expanded, bus routes were added to take visitors directly to these locales, and the Pagoda embarked on another career as a garden center. It served as a venue for a wide variety of garden clubs' meetings, as well as an indoor facility for garden shows, particularly the long run of the annual Point Defiance Park "Gardeners' Paradise Days," established by Director of Horticulture Howard Harmon, who served the park district in the 1950s and 1960s.

A major restoration in 1988 extended the public life of the Pagoda, and it joined the nearby Lodge serving as an additional popular rental facility in Point Defiance Park for weddings, corporate meetings, and other social functions. In this capacity, the Pagoda made memories of all kinds for the next quarter of a century. In this photograph from August 1992, Brett and Melanie Freshwaters celebrate their wedding at the Pagoda with family and friends. The life of the beloved park landmark was seriously threatened by arson in 2011, but the well-built structure survived and, after careful restoration throughout 2012, continues to serve as a locale for graceful gatherings. (Courtesy Brett and Melanie Freshwaters.)

Located adjacent to the Pagoda and across the road from the Lodge, the three tennis courts have been a fixture in Point Defiance Park since 1910, when the park board authorized their construction. Originally, they were surfaced with coke and tar. Tennis racquets and balls were available at the Pagoda's retail counter. Here, a couple of players return to the picnic ground from the courts.

On September 25, 1915, the Mary Ball Chapter of the Daughters of the American Revolution placed a monument to Charles Wilkes and the US Exploring Expedition of 1838–1842 near the Lodge and the tennis courts, which was where Wilkes was believed to have landed in 1841. Park visitors Tim Christie, Maria Sampen, and their dog, Sarastro, visit the spot in 2012. (Courtesy Terri Walton.)

In November 1898, the Board of Park Commissioners petitioned the US secretary of war for a relic from the USS *Maine*, the sinking of which in Havana Harbor earlier that year launched the Spanish-American War. At a grand unveiling on Memorial Day in 1913, a shell was installed on a base with a commemorative bronze tablet, near the site of today's Japanese Garden. (Courtesy WSHS.)

The location of the USS *Maine* memorial near the Pagoda has not changed in almost a century. However, the site today is no longer the well-travelled path taken by most visitors who arrived by streetcar and paused by the memorial to "*Remember the Maine!*" on their way down to the Point Defiance waterfront. (Courtesy Christine Dennett.)

Two

"Handsome Ferneries, Golden Glories, and a Velvet Sward"

The *Tacoma Sunday Ledger* of April 30, 1899, could be forgiven for its effusive praise of the gardens and landscaping finally taking hold in Point Defiance under the direction of Superintendent Ebenezer Roberts and his crew of landscape artists. Even in the early days, the gardens of Point Defiance Park inspired, delighted, and taught. That legacy continues.

With more recent additions in outlying areas, the gardens of Point Defiance Park have a long history in the developed acreage nearest the park's main entrance. Felling native stands of timber to carve a genteel landscape out of Northwest forests was not without controversy, even in the early years. But the consensus more than a century ago supported limiting such deliberate horticulture to the southern area of Point Defiance, where the elevation could be most easily reached, altered, and managed. Thus, the lower area to the left of the main park entrance, which tended to be marshy, was cleared to form a pond. Adjacent acreage was turned to the tasks of animal husbandry, with elk and bison pens, as well as to introducing some of the early features of park gardens such as a large bulb cultivation field. The creation of the first rose garden dates from as early as 1895, when Ebenezer Roberts solicited donations of rose cuttings from local schoolchildren. Three years later, the *Tacoma Daily Ledger* of August 7, 1898, detailed 75 varieties of roses thriving in the park as a result of his appeal.

In the decades since the indefatigable Roberts, additional gardens specializing in Northwest native species, and others featuring herb, fuchsia, dahlia, iris, and rhododendron exemplars have developed in dedicated areas of the park, bridging generations with the pleasures of cultivation as well as ever-evolving lessons in horticultural stewardship.

Ebenezer Rhys Roberts (1854–1918) cleared and planted much of Point Defiance Park's formal lawn and garden areas when he worked for Tacoma's fledgling system of parks from 1890 until his retirement as superintendent in 1908. Photographs of him in these years always show a spade or wheelbarrow close at hand. (Courtesy Jean Insel Robeson.)

This 1892 image, turned into a postcard, records Roberts's early handiwork with what could be planted, as well as with what could not be easily cleared. "Every great stump has been hollowed at the top to plant vines and flowers," enthused the *Tacoma Sunday Ledger* of April 30, 1899, in admiration of Roberts's efforts.

Both of these c. 1910 views of the entry area of Point Defiance Park illustrate the close coexistence of the exhibited flora and fauna. Pens for the animals of the early zoological collection—such as elk, deer, and ostrich—stood adjacent to a two-and-a-half-acre hyacinth bulb farm. The farm later gave way to an expanse of lawn and flowerbeds that were a challenge to keep alive in the summer months without a ready supply of fresh water. One of the suggestions of the Hare & Hare Plan of 1911 was to remove the animal husbandry aspects of the park farther up the hill and out of the entry bowl area. (Above image courtesy TPL.)

The solution to the lack of an adequate water supply in Point Defiance Park was construction in 1899 of a water tank and powerhouse built over a new well supplied with a five-horsepower pump, worked by an electric generator of 15 horsepower. The water tank was located not far from the Lodge and soon fed 1,500 feet of pipes to keep the gardens watered.

Another water feature close to the Lodge and the well was a pond that Ebenezer Roberts developed in the small yard area off the turreted verandah side of his park residence. Featuring a rustic bridge and lily pads, the pond charmed park visitors with small fountains, also made possible by construction of the water tank.

Stepping out from his home in the Keeper's Lodge around 1906, Ebenezer Roberts would have seen this view of the Point Defiance Park greenhouse. The Hare & Hare Plan of 1911 would later take issue with the practice of scattered floral beds, such as those in the foreground. (Courtesy Jean Insel Robeson.)

Sections of the entry to Point Defiance Park, which modern visitors know as the vast expanse of lawn surrounding the bowl area, once served as a planting ground for seedlings and bedding plants. The new water tank and well apparatus of 1899 are visible at far right, while zoological pens occupy the slope at the top left.

This image illustrates the scattered ornamental bedding of annuals that the Hare & Hare Plan of 1911 found indiscriminate and expensive to maintain. Their plan advocated limiting such beds, proffering instead a planting design that they held would not "detract from the restfulness of the landscape."

The view down the Rose Arbor at Point Defiance Park has remained reassuringly the same for decades. Originally, spokes of rose arbor walks emanated in several directions, delighting the senses of young and old.

Styles in women's fashion change over the decades, but the Point Defiance Park Rose Arbor endures. These two views, separated by perhaps 50 years, show the expanse down the length of the same arbor. The above photograph, from around 1905, shows the spokes' central junction at the far end of the tunnel of roses, as well as flowerbeds flanking the arbor's sides. The woman may be Ebenezer Roberts's wife, Mary Ann, as it is a family photograph. The below image, from 1953, shows Dee Fitzgerald inspecting the bedding plants in a flower bed now oriented down the center of the arbor. She was featured in a series of poses in several gardens in Point Defiance for a newspaper article entitled "Beautiful Parks." (Above image courtesy Jean Insel Robeson.)

The Rose Arbor, while a central and abiding feature of the gardens at Point Defiance Park, was not the only interesting horticultural attraction. In this early postcard image, park visitors stroll past the circular Canna Bed, where the arbors of climbing roses intersected. The canna is a flowering tropical perennial, favorable then and now to the temperate climate of the Northwest.

A hydrangea bed beckoned appreciative inspection in the spring of 1913. The structures at center left are some of the early buildings housing the zoological collections. In this era, animal shelters and gardens were interspersed throughout the park's entry grounds.

Arches of ivy were popular features dotted throughout the grounds of Point Defiance Park, many originally planted to climb the stumps and upturned roots left in place after the early years of clearing trees to make way for flowerbeds. The Hare & Hare Plan of 1911 actually advocated planting English ivy throughout the park. Their report to the Board of Park Commissioners described the tenacious vine as "most satisfactory for walls, tree trunks, stumps and steep banks," an example of just how much horticultural wisdom and practice has evolved over the past century, in terms of dealing with invasive species. These two postcards actually show opposite sides of the same ivy arch, though on the below image, the printer has mistakenly rendered the word ivy as "ivory."

The evolution of Point Defiance Park's horticultural landscape is noted in these wide-angle views of the entry bowl area, both taken from a similar vantage point near the park's sloping hillside exit road. As seen in the above image from around 1910, the animal shelters and the greenhouse dominated in the early 20th century, with nary an automobile in the scene. By 1939, however, as the below image shows, there are maturing deciduous trees and a broader expanse of manicured lawn. As advocated by the Hare & Hare Plan of 1911, the animal shelters have been removed farther uphill, which separated zoological and horticultural functions and also provided a more permanent roadbed for the increasing presence of the personal vehicle. (Below courtesy TPL.)

Distinguished visitors to the city were often invited to plant trees and ornamental bushes and shrubs in Tacoma's parks. Surrounded by a sea of fashionable cloche hats, world-famous Austrian-born opera singer Ernestine Schumann-Heink (1861–1936) planted a rose bush in a new section of the Point Defiance Park rose garden in May 1928. Newspaper coverage of the occasion noted that the flower was "an Edouard Herriot rose grafted on a prairie sweetbrier." The staked sign on the ground reads "zur Erinnerung," German for "in commemoration" of Mme. Schumann-Heink's visit. She was on a nationwide tour in 1928. Flanking the honored park visitor are park arborist Hiram DePuy (left), and park board president James Hays. (Courtesy TPL.)

Howard Harmon, director of horticulture for the Metropolitan Park District of Tacoma, inspects the damage to the Point Defiance Park rose garden in March 1956 following a devastating freeze the previous November. According to park board meeting minutes of January 1956, Harmon feared the total loss of the park's signature rose beds.

The rose gardens had to be replanted following the November 1955 freeze. In this photograph from March 1956, work crews dig the beds for thousands of dollars' worth of new roses paid for by park district contingency funds and community contributions. Reminiscent of Ebenezer Roberts's appeal to schoolchildren for rose cuttings 60 years earlier, scout troops stepped up with their pennies to help the rose gardens following the freeze.

The All-America Rose Selections (AARS) nonprofit association, formed in 1938, selected the Point Defiance Park Rose Garden as one of the earliest to be accredited as a designated display garden. When the AARS withdrew this distinction in 1986, at a low point in the rose garden's fortunes, the Tacoma Rose Society mobilized its membership for hundreds of hours of re-accreditation labor. On July 21, 1990, the Point Defiance Park Rose Garden was rededicated with a new central gazebo. In the foreground, park commissioners Debbie Regala and Peter Norman celebrate the occasion. There are now upwards of 1,500 rose bushes, as well as miniature and climbing roses, on more than an acre of land. The gazebo hosts many a summer wedding and offers a fragrant and shady haven for park visitors.

From the early 1890s, photographs clearly document the clearing and draining of the naturally marshy area at the bottom of the sloping topography at the park's entrance. One early newspaper article called it "a great cedar swamp, waist-deep and covering two-and-one-half acres during the rainy season." By 1900, the vestigial swamp had become a pastoral pond with fountains and ornamental water plants. These two images from October 1972 document the construction of the pond's artfully created features that remain familiar to today's park visitors. In the above photograph, a rustic bridge leads to a series of island pathways. The image below documents the substructure of the pond's man-made waterfall, which now cascades off the overhanging ledge at the right of the structure that was disguised under earth, rocks, and plants by the end of the project.

After the long run of the Point Defiance Gardeners' Paradise Days, held in the park from the late 1950s through the early 1970s, a large-scale horticultural event was revived during the summers of 2005 through 2007. The Point Defiance Flower & Garden Show covered some 12 acres of the park's gardens and bowl area each summer. Exhibits included Grand Display Gardens, children's pavilions, window box and container gardens, advice and lectures on innumerable horticultural topics, fine musical entertainment, and gourmet food and drink. The above photograph captures the flavor of the many specialty booths; below, a life-size cut-out portrait (see page 12) of the park's original gardener, Ebenezer Rhys Roberts, presided over the spirit of the 2005 event.

During the summers of the Point Defiance Flower & Garden Show, various contestants in the container garden category dotted the lawns surrounding the Lodge, a historical nod to Ebenezer Roberts's early use of container gardening to add spots of color to the park. The winner of the 2005 Best in Show poses proudly in front of Roberts's original home in Point Defiance.

The cut flower arrangements exhibited in the Pagoda during the Point Defiance Flower & Garden Show hearkened back to its use in the 1960s and 1970s for floral displays of all kinds. Behind the flower enthusiasts, panels from the 2005 Point Defiance Park centennial exhibit provided historical context for a century of horticultural accomplishment.

Three

"The Park's Greatest Treasure" —The Waterfront

"The park's greatest treasure was its beach and waterfront," wrote Trillium Roberts Insel in her reminiscences of growing up in Point Defiance Park.

Bordered on three sides by the tidal waters of Puget Sound, it is only natural that the Point Defiance waterfront has always been a popular gathering place. For centuries, Native Americans used its beaches as campsites as they traveled Puget Sound by canoe, fished the "skookum" waters for salmon, or dug for clams along its shore.

Early settlers to the area soon discovered the beauty of the Point Defiance waterfront, reaching it by boat, horse, or trail. Once the streetcar line to the park was completed in 1890, visitors thronged to the shore to picnic, walk the beach, and enjoy a refreshing summer breeze off the always cool waters of Puget Sound. For a short period of time, the Board of Park Commissioners even allowed vacationers to reserve campsites along the beach.

To accommodate the growing demand for waterfront amenities, a small dock, bait shop, and fruit stand were built along the shore. Over the years, a succession of four boathouse pavilions have graced the Point Defiance waterfront, providing moorage for boats, refreshments, fishing and picnic supplies, boat rentals, and more. These pavilions became natural gathering spots for waterfront entertainment such as the Tacoma Yacht Club's Bathing Girl Revues in the 1920s, the Water Carnivals of the 1930s and 1940s, and fishing derbies too numerous to count.

The pleasure of strolling the waterfront from the boathouse to the tip of Point Defiance, picnicking along the promenade, or playing in the brisk water at Owen Beach has drawn generations of people to the beauty of the waters of Puget Sound to enjoy "the park's greatest treasure."

Before there were any permanent structures along the waterfront, Edwin Ferris and Gage Wheeler, owners of the Tacoma Boat House, transported summer campers and equipment from their South Tenth Street location to Point Defiance aboard their passenger steamer, the *Mockingbird*. Campers recognized the *Mockingbird*'s familiar steam calliope whistle and knew when the boat was bringing supplies and other vacationers, though not everyone appreciated the whistle's piercing sound.

The first public amenities in Point Defiance were built upon the waterfront. As early as 1895, the park commissioners agreed to lease property for a boat stand, floats upon the shore, bait stand, fruit stand, and restaurant for $5 per month. Three years later, Edwin Ferris won the contract with an offer of $85 per year and took over the boathouse operation. (Courtesy Robin Paterson.)

Edwin Ferris and his wife, Edith, built a concession stand near the site of today's boathouse marina. From the small rustic structure, they rented boats and sold foods for picnics. Edith jokingly referred to the building as "the shack." A float with a narrow walkway extended into the bay to accommodate boats. Profits from the boat and concession business soon demonstrated the need for a more elaborate building. (Courtesy WSHS.)

In 1902, the park board entered into a contract with Ferris to build a restaurant and pavilion at his own expense in exchange for a 10-year contract to operate refreshment and boat-rental concessions at the park. Opening on June 13, 1903, the pavilion's only access was by boat or on pathways leading down from the park's streetcar stop. The structure in the foreground is a rig for driving pilings for the dock. (Courtesy Robin Paterson.)

The Ferris Boathouse Pavilion was an imposing octagonal structure 60 feet in diameter with a covered porch extending out an additional 16 feet. The pavilion contained a restaurant and stands for penny candy, ice cream, refreshing ices, and roasted peanuts. The upper floor served as the Ferris family residence. The facility also included a substantial boat landing and, underneath, a spacious boathouse where boats could be rented for a day of fishing.

The popularity of the new pavilion resulted in the addition of a second streetcar line to the park. Steamers also made daily excursions between downtown Tacoma and the pavilion. In the restaurant, white linens graced tables set among potted palms. Each morning, a man from Vashon Island delivered fresh clams for the specialty of the house: Mrs. Ferris's delicious clam chowder.

In addition to the restaurant, the Ferris boathouse ran a booming business renting rowboats, which were stored in the lower level below the pavilion. The popular tradition of renting boats at the boathouse continues today. During a trip to the park in 1920, five-year-old Patricia Quinn poses for the camera in one of the park's rental boats. (Courtesy Susan Delisle.)

Killian Van R. Schermerhorn (in boat) and Wilmot McCune spent a week rowing 80 nautical miles from Point Defiance to Olympia and back in a double-oared boat they rented from the Point Defiance boathouse in August 1926. The Stadium High School juniors stayed close to shore or hopped from island to island, camping when they needed rest. (Courtesy TPL.)

As business continued to grow, the Board of Park Commissioners decided that a larger, more substantial boathouse was needed. In 1918, architects A.J. Russell and E.N. Dugan were hired to design the building. Their design included a center tower with an observation deck 140 feet above the main floor. The right wing would contain a restaurant, dance floor, boat storage, and boat rentals. The left wing was to be the home of a new indoor swimming pool.

Realizing that it did not have the money to build the entire new pavilion at one time, the park board planned to build it in units as funding became available. In 1919, construction began on the first floor of the right wing of the new pavilion, adjacent to the existing octagonal pavilion. The large concrete structure with graceful arching entryways became the new boat storage and boat repair facility.

When the first floor of the new boathouse pavilion was completed in 1921, the top deck was finished with detailed railings and lighting to accommodate evening affairs. To celebrate completion of this phase of the project, a dinner was held on the new platform with live music for the evening's entertainment.

The second and third stories of the new pavilion were added in 1925–1926. The structure complemented the functions in the old pavilion with a new kitchen, lunch rooms, public meeting spaces, and open decks. During the 1930s, the third floor of the pavilion was converted to employee housing. Then, during World War II, this area became the home of the crash boat crews of the US Army Air Corps.

The interior of the new pavilion, shown here decorated for Easter in 1930, was a delightful spot to enjoy a leisurely meal while visiting the park. The main dining area opened all the way up to the third floor, which was ringed with walkways and enclosed meeting spaces and housing. (Courtesy TPL.)

The new boathouse pavilion drew even larger crowds to the waterfront. The rising popularity of the automobile also required that parking lots be added near the pavilion to accommodate those now driving instead of using the streetcar. Before the planned second wing of the pavilion and observation tower was built, the country plunged into the Great Depression, and they were never constructed.

In 1933, a small trial aquarium was set up on the main floor of the pavilion. It was an instant success, and within three years the park board approved building an additional 20 tanks for display purposes and to expand the operating hours to provide opportunities for school classes to visit. Watching the seal exhibit, especially Dub Dub, was a highlight for all visitors.

John Slipp, manager and aquarist of the Point Defiance aquarium, stands next to one of the displays he created in 1948. Slipp was named "Young Man of 1947" by the Junior Chamber of Commerce. More than 82,000 people visited the park's aquarium in 1947. The aquarium left its waterfront location and moved its exhibits to the zoo in 1963. (Courtesy TPL.)

During the 1930s, the Works Progress Administration (WPA) undertook many improvement projects in Point Defiance Park. Their last major undertaking was the construction of a new boathouse pavilion on the location where Edwin Ferris's octagonal pavilion once stood. In poor condition, Ferris's pavilion was torn down in 1933. The grand opening of the new WPA pavilion was held on June 9, 1940. This new Point Defiance Boathouse and Pavilion was said to be the largest boathouse west of Chicago. It was built at a cost of $32,000 and used 150,000 feet of lumber cut and milled in the park. The upper area housed a concession shop, restaurant, and lunch counter. The bottom level was used for boat storage.

The WPA boathouse was modified and enlarged in 1947 and again in 1962 to keep up with public demand for good food on the waterfront and fishing supplies. Ralph Tachell, seen here in his starched white uniform, started working at the restaurant and concession stand in 1956. He was still running the facility at the time it was destroyed by an arsonist's fire in 1984.

When completed, the lower level of the boathouse contained 500 boat lockers, where individuals could store their personal boats, making it very convenient to get out on the water quickly when the fishing was good. There was also space for an additional 200 concession boats and 50 lockers specifically designed for the storage of motor boats.

The boathouse and pavilion were often the location for many community events, such as the annual Water Carnivals sponsored by the Young Men's Business Club. The carnivals drew thousands of visitors to the waterfront to watch the tugboat races, swimming competitions, and many other water-related activities.

This aerial photograph of the Boat House and Pavilion, taken in August 1948, illustrates the size and scale of the larger bottom floor utilized for boat storage and the variety of docking options for people visiting the facility by boat. The upper two floors of the older 1925 pavilion were destroyed by fire in 1974, but the concrete first floor prevented the fire from reaching the new boathouse.

The WPA Boat House and Pavilion escaped the earlier fire that destroyed the 1925 pavilion, but a three-alarm arson fire destroyed the entire complex in September 1984, including an estimated 250 private boats stored in the boat lockers at the time.

After the fire, the boating and fishing community rallied to encourage the park board to build yet another boathouse on the waterfront. Today's Point Defiance Marina Complex opened in the spring of 1988. In addition to new boat lockers, tackle shop, and gas pumps, an octagon-shaped restaurant was built to honor the first boathouse, and the concrete first floor of the 1925 boathouse is still used for boat storage.

The Nereides Baths was Tacoma's first indoor swimming pool. It was located on the bluff overlooking the Point Defiance ferry landing. The name Nereides referred to sea goddesses in Greek mythology who gave aid to sailors. Designed by noted Tacoma architect Frederick Heath, the baths opened on Memorial Day 1906. Swimmers enjoyed a 50-by-150-foot pool with water pumped from Puget Sound and heated to 80 degrees by a wood-burning furnace; amenities included a diving board, slide, dressing rooms, and spectator gallery. Originally planned as a year-round facility, it soon became a summertime-only attraction. Over time, the combination of an aging wooden building exposed to humid saltwater and changing sanitary regulations forced the facility's closure. Several other options were discussed for its use, such as an ice-skating rink, but in the end, it was demolished in 1932.

September 3, 1925, was J.T. Richmond's 80th birthday. Better known as "Dad," he spent the day hard at work at the Nereides Baths, teaching beginners how to swim. Dad was believed to be the oldest water sports instructor in the nation. Five-year-old Charlotte Hannah was his student in this photograph. (Courtesy TPL.)

Included with the cost of admission to the Nereides Baths was the rental of a navy blue, one-piece woven wool bathing suit. New suits were ordered each year from the Olympia Knitting Company. One challenging aspect of these suits is that they tended to stretch and cling when they got wet and well worn, requiring the swimmers to make frequent adjustments for modesty's sake. (Courtesy John Lisicich.)

A crowd of more than 2,000 people jammed the pavilion and lined the beach to watch the finish of the first channel swim from Vashon Island (Talequah) to Point Defiance on September 26, 1926. The two-mile swim was won by Gerhard Bahr (third from left above) in a time of one hour and two minutes. Even greater cheers erupted when the lone female in the competition, Alexina Slater, a 15-year-old high school student (fifth from left), came in fourth. Of the 12 swimmers who started the race, two had to be rescued by boat before reaching the finish.

A huge crowd gathered on the docks, floats, and boat ramps of the Point Defiance Pavilion to watch the parade of beautiful women participating in the Tacoma Yacht Club's Bathing Girl Revue on July 4, 1924. As seen in the above photograph, two intrepid young men even climbed out of a second-floor window of the pavilion in order to get a better look. A policeman is in the foreground, presumably hired to maintain order at the event. Instead, his attention appears to be focused on the contestants below. A close-up view of several contestants can be seen on the cover of this book. As this picture illustrates, this was still an era when a day at the park meant hats, jackets, and ties for men. (Courtesy TPL.)

The first Young Men's Business Club Water Carnival was held in 1938. The success led to it becoming an annual event, with thousands filling the pavilion to enjoy the festivities. On July 16, 1939, the highlights of the day included an exhibition of logrolling and a five-man boat race, and ended with a thrilling tugboat race from Crab Point to the pavilion. (Courtesy TPL.)

The 1940 Water Carnival featured boating competitions in a variety of categories: inboard motors, hydroplanes, outboard motors, and sailboats. In this photograph, the speedboats get ready for their race. With names like *Blood and Bones*, *Poison Ivy*, and *Oomph*, these boats and their drivers were ready to tackle the waters of Puget Sound. (Courtesy TPL.)

The new Point Defiance to Gig Harbor ferry, *Defiance*, started service on April 3, 1927. The 180-foot wooden ferry was constructed of Douglas fir and had a capacity of 70 cars and 500 foot passengers. Built by the Skansie Shipbuilding Company in Gig Harbor, the new ferry was designed to speed up traffic between Tacoma and Gig Harbor. (Courtesy TPL.)

During the Water Carnival on June 30, 1940, these four men sold tickets for the last ferry ride across the Narrows. The grand opening of the Narrows Bridge was held on July 1, 1940. The following day, 1,400 people purchased tickets for the ferry *Kalakala*'s final trip across the water. The passengers danced to the music of Louis Nomellini's orchestra on their way to Gig Harbor. (Courtesy TPL.)

Geraldine Stiltner was the big winner in the "Dad and Daughter" division of the 11th Annual Tacoma Poggie Club Salmon Derby held on July 25, 1948. Her king salmon, weighing 14 pounds and two ounces, won her a new girl's bicycle. A record-breaking 296 children competed that year, and 100 salmon were caught. (Courtesy TPL.)

Contestants in the 1944 Fishermen's Derby for boys and girls, sponsored by the Tacoma Poggie Club, show off their catches as they await the presentation of awards. The person catching the largest salmon won a new bicycle. Other prizes included dart boards and baseball bats, gloves, and balls. (Courtesy TPL.)

All along the shore of Point Defiance Park runs a beautiful sandy beach. Early in the park's history, people would spend their summers camped upon the shore. After Edwin Ferris built his octagonal Boathouse Pavilion in 1903, the crowds would often spend part of their day walking the waterfront looking for treasures while enjoying the cool breezes off Puget Sound.

The beach walk was so popular that the Hare & Hare Master Plan of 1911 recommended building a formal promenade from the pavilion to the area now called Owen Beach. Beginning in 1916, construction began on the promenade and continued at a rate of 600 feet per year over a five-year period. Once the promenade was completed, walkers no longer had to worry about the whims of the tide to ensure dry feet.

Once the promenade was complete in 1921, the area known as "new beach" or "picnic beach" became an even more popular destination. Additional work by the WPA in the 1930s added a road down to the beach from Five Mile Drive, a Bathhouse and concession building, and a log shelter that served as a community kitchen.

The beach area was given a formal title in 1959, when it was named Owen Beach to honor 47-year Metro Parks Tacoma employee Floyd E. Owen. Owen worked in the parks from 1912 to 1959. For many of those years, he served as the superintendent of parks and lived in the Point Defiance Lodge. Owen (far right) is seen here receiving a plaque honoring his first 42 years of service.

Four

A Splendid Collection of Birds and Animals

Today's internationally renowned and award-winning Point Defiance Zoo & Aquarium grew from humble beginnings. In 1891, the animal collection consisted of two deer and a possum. It was not long before people began donating a variety of new species to the park. According to early park superintendent Ebenezer Roberts, "Tacoma being a seaport makes the collection of animals a comparatively easy task and many fine specimens can be obtained from vessels making this port from foreign lands." Soon, there were bears, monkeys, lions, kangaroos, and pheasants on display, followed by herds of elk, deer, and buffalo corralled in pens abutting the walkways of the garden area. A 1904 article in the *Tacoma Daily Ledger* declared that "Point Defiance is becoming the home of a rare zoological exhibit."

In the early decades of the 20th century, the zoo was located lower in the park than its present uphill location, with the buffalo pen standing in what is now the entry bowl area of the park. The 1911 Hare & Hare Plan for the park suggested that the buffalo and elk pens be removed from the bowl area to make way for lawns and a drive. The plan also supported a substantial increase in the zoological collection in the park and recommended building new animal enclosures to house the growing collection. Eventual improvements to the zoo dating from the vision of Hare & Hare included a new barn for elk in 1913 and a new Pheasantry in 1914, both of which exhibited the rustic Japanese-style architecture advocated by Hare & Hare.

Over the years, a wide variety of animals have called Point Defiance home, and many of them became beloved celebrities in the community. In the early years, there were black bears Jack and Mollie, and Peggy the sacred baboon of India. In more recent times, Dub Dub the harbor seal, Cindy the elephant, and E.T. the walrus reached superstar status.

Just as important are the successful conservation and education efforts of the Point Defiance Zoo & Aquarium. Generations of children have learned to appreciate wildlife, and species such as the Red wolf and Clouded leopard have benefited from successful breeding programs, thanks to knowledgeable and dedicated staff and volunteers.

As the animal collection grew to include herds of deer, elk, and buffalo in the early years of the 20th century, large pens were constructed in the area near the entry bowl of the park. Shelters were constructed in each area to provide feeding stations for the animals. The park's early greenhouse can be seen at right in this photograph.

Realizing that the zoo's bear collection needed more secure enclosures, park officials built exhibit cages specifically designed for the bears in 1899 and 1905. Even with tall iron bars, bears were known to escape from time to time. One of the grizzly bears escaped in 1938 and roamed the north end of Tacoma for almost three weeks before he was captured and returned to the zoo.

One of the two Alaskan brown bears entertains visitors to the park shortly after the new exhibit was constructed in 1905. This bear cage was removed from the park in 2002 to make room for the zoo's Wild Wonders Outdoor Theater.

The park's first superintendent, Ebenezer Roberts, raised two black bear cubs, Jack and Mollie, to adulthood as one of his many responsibilities. They were followed by several generations of black bears on exhibit. The early cages allowed visitors to get close enough to feed the bears through the bars. The enclosures included small pools and tree trunks for the bears to get some much-needed exercise after all the treats.

At one time, the zoo had a sizeable herd of elk. When Pres. Theodore Roosevelt visited Tacoma in 1903, he was given a unique chair made from six sets of antlers from a Point Defiance elk. Park superintendent Ebenezer Roberts (at right in the left photograph) collected the antlers each year as they were shed by the elk and worked with local taxidermist Fred Edwards to fashion them into a chair for the president. The chair weighed 150 pounds and was valued at $1,000 at the time. Many visitors to the park at the turn of the century were entertained by another bull elk, named Dewey. Dewey was famous for running around his pen carrying large logs in his antlers that had been placed there for his enjoyment. (Courtesy of Jean Insel Robeson.)

Dressed for a summer outing, visitors to the park's early zoological collections in the 1890s admire the monkeys in their shelter. The sign on the shed reads, "The people are requested not to torment the animals." (Courtesy WSHS.)

In 1914, a new Pheasantry was built. Following the suggestions from the 1911 Hare & Hare Plan, the building exhibited the same rustic Japanese architecture as the new streetcar station built that year. Note the decorative elements of the roofline that mimic those of the Pagoda. A raised section was also added to accommodate large birds, such as the bald eagle seen here sitting on a perch.

When a small herd of buffalo arrived at Point Defiance from Montana in 1908, they were said to be the first bison brought west of the Rocky Mountains. Initially, the buffalo pen was near the entrance to the park. In 1912, it was relocated farther up the hill, in the vicinity of today's zoo parking lot. The buffalo exhibit closed in 1930.

In February 1914, early Washington pioneer Ezra Meeker (right) donated his two oxen, Dave and Dandy, to the zoo. Meeker and the oxen had traveled the Oregon Trail to promote the importance of remembering its historical significance. The oxen were to live out their retirement with the park's buffalo herd. After they died later that year, they were taxidermed and given to the Washington State Historical Society for display. (Courtesy WSHS.)

Oscar Olson served as zookeeper for more than 33 years. He is seen here in 1927 weighing Jeff, a tiny ring-tailed monkey. Tipping the scales at three pounds, Jeff, declared Olson, needed to go on a diet. Olson's job as "chef" for the animals at the zoo earned him the number 11 ranking among "Tacoma's Strangest Jobs." (Courtesy TPL.)

On April 9, 1926, a baby baboon known as the "sacred baboon of India" was born at the zoo. Her parents were purchased from a circus the year before. She was named Peggy and quickly became the greatest attraction at the zoo. Unfortunately, shortly after her first birthday, Peggy died after eating a cherry that someone had placed in her cage.

Zookeeper George Jones poses with Jocko, a spider monkey from South America. Jocko chattered constantly and quickly learned to imitate human behaviors, such as washing his face and hands. He was a great favorite with zoogoers in the 1930s. (Courtesy TPL.)

This small monkey elicited great interest from the zoo's big cats when he visited the animal house. Here a tiger intently watches as the monkey talks up a storm. It is lucky for him that the tiger is behind thick glass. In the shadows to the right, a jaguar was also paying close attention to their visitor.

In 1953, a new animal house (above) opened at the zoo to replace an outdated and dilapidated facility. Due to the conditions at the old animal house, the park board made plans to move the lions to Seattle's Woodland Park Zoo. On the day in 1951 that the truck arrived to take the lions away, a group of women led by Mrs. Dale Graham besieged the director of the Woodland Park Zoo, and he retreated to Seattle without the lions. The group began a fundraising effort to build the new animal house in Point Defiance. When it opened, it housed three lions, a cougar, a jaguar, and two white-faced gibbons. Below, a grateful lion appears to be letting the keeper know that she is happy with her new quarters.

In 1959, a new exhibit called the Children's Farm was added. The 4H and the Future Farmers of America provided the workers as well as the animals. Originally open only during the summer months, the animals went back to their owners in the fall. In addition to pony rides, there was a petting zoo where children could feed and touch goats, chickens, and ducks.

As part of a major upgrade and expansion of the zoo in 2005, the old Children's Farm and Petting Zoo was replaced with a lively and engaging Kid's Zone. The area was designed for children to learn through touch, exploration, and movement, such as climbing like a gecko. There is even a water play area for warm, sunny days.

In 1963, thirty years after an aquarium opened on the waterfront, a new marine facility was built at the zoo. The name of the zoo was changed to Point Defiance Zoo & Aquarium (PDZA) to reflect the addition of these new exhibits. This 50,000-gallon aquarium, now called the North Pacific Aquarium, exhibits local sea life such as salmon, rockfish, and giant Pacific octopus.

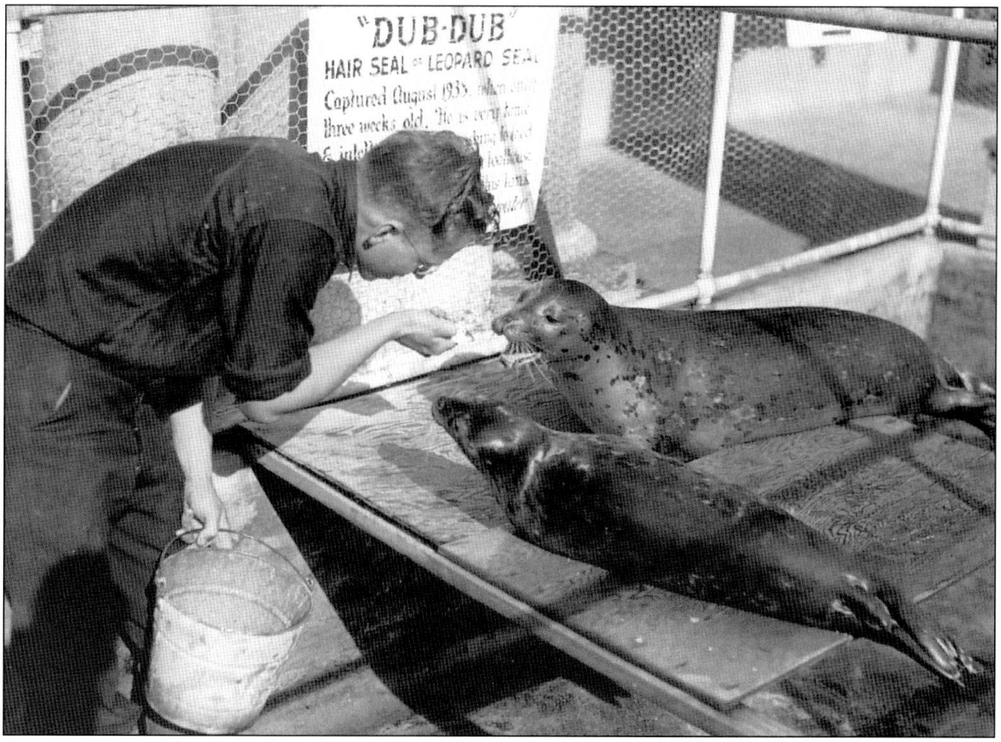

When the waterfront aquarium closed, its most popular exhibit, Dub Dub the harbor seal, moved up the hill to the new facility at the zoo. Dub Dub was donated to the park in 1938 and quickly won the hearts of all with his crowd-pleasing antics. He is seen here with Fifi the Second being fed by aquarist Wilhelm Jordan. Dub Dub died in 1972 at age 33. A bronze statue of Dub Dub honors his memory.

Polar bears were added to the zoo's animal collection in 1921, when two cubs were purchased for $500. The park board opted to remodel the old 1905 bear exhibit area for the new polar bears. Polar bears were still using this aging and inadequate facility until 1980, when a new award-winning polar bear complex was completed. The new exhibit included an 11-foot-deep saltwater pool with an underground viewing area for visitors to go nose-to-nose with these beautiful animals. Today, three polar bears, Blizzard, Glacier, and Boris, continue to entertain and amaze park visitors. Blizzard and Glacier came to the zoo as cubs in 1997. Boris was rescued from a circus in 2002.

In 1965, one of the zoo's most famous residents arrived—Cindy the Asian elephant. Cindy was three years old and weighed 3,000 pounds at the time. She is seen here with keeper Rich Johnson. On her 40th birthday, in 2002, Cindy's cake consisted of hay, apples, carrots, bananas, melons, pears, and strawberries. She died later that year. A new elephant barn was dedicated to her memory in 2003.

The zoo acquired two baby African elephants, Moyo and Thandi, in 1983. They are seen here with keepers Jeff Zimmerman (left) and Gary Miller. The two elephants stayed at the zoo until 1997, when they were sold to Disney's Animal Kingdom at Walt Disney World for the park's fledgling elephant-breeding program. While there, Moyo gave birth to two calves.

From 1970 to 1981, the Betts family operated a popular carousel ride at the zoo (above). Built in 1906 by the C.W. Parker Carousel Factory, the ride had 36 wooden horses and was originally powered by a steam engine. Byron Betts relocated the carousel to Enchanted Village in Federal Way in 1981. Twenty five years later, the zoo once again featured a carousel. This time, it was a 1917 C.W. Parker two-row carousel featuring hand-carved animals created by the Washington Antique Carousel Society (below). The group devoted more than 25,000 hours to creating 28 large and 3 small animals, a sled, and other adornments. The carousel's outer ring features horses with Washington State themes. The inner ring has endangered species and Northwest native animals, including a husky, a cougar, and a slug.

A core mission of the zoo is the conservation of animal species. The red wolf had nearly vanished from the wild in the 1970s. By 1980, the last 14 pure wolves were brought to PDZA as part of a highly successful breeding and recovery program to bring the species back from the brink of extinction. Today, over 250 are alive, many of which have been reintroduced into the wild.

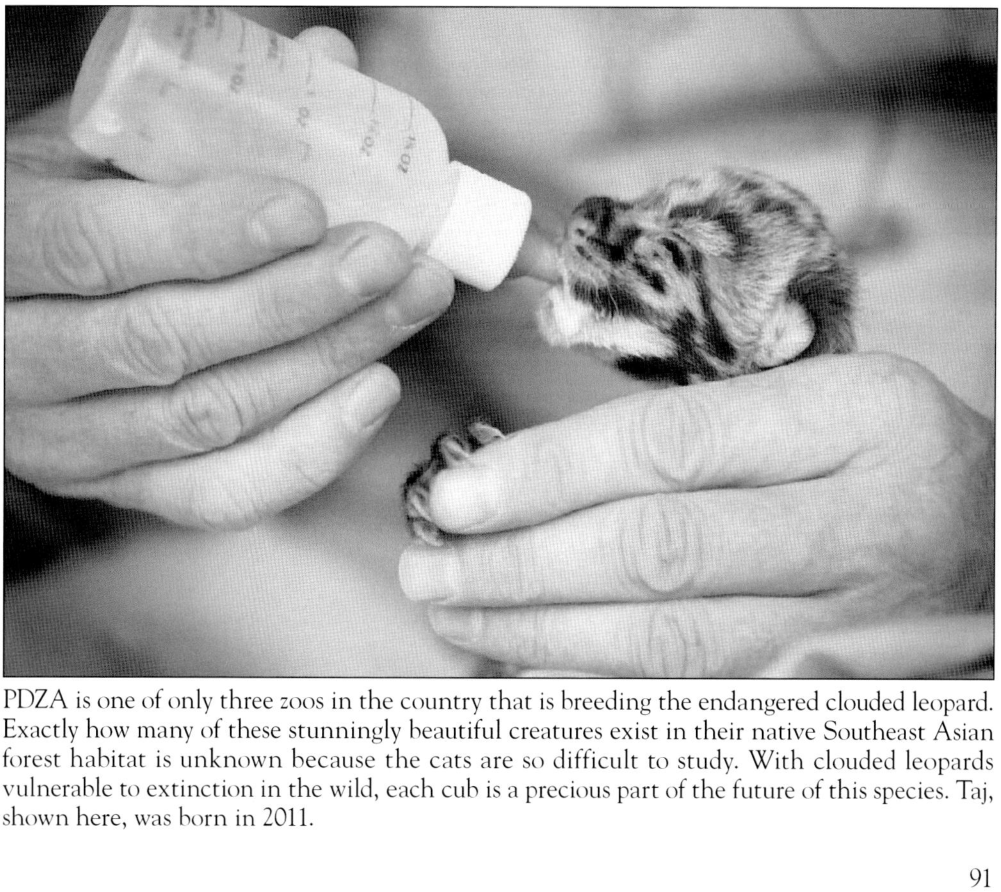

PDZA is one of only three zoos in the country that is breeding the endangered clouded leopard. Exactly how many of these stunningly beautiful creatures exist in their native Southeast Asian forest habitat is unknown because the cats are so difficult to study. With clouded leopards vulnerable to extinction in the wild, each cub is a precious part of the future of this species. Taj, shown here, was born in 2011.

In addition to species conservation, education is another core mission of the zoo. Above, the Marine Discovery Center offers a variety of hands-on opportunities for budding scientists to learn more about marine life. Below, Whitney Crittenden is one of the staff members who interact with zoo visitors, showcasing special ambassador animals, such as this eagle owl, to provide "close encounters" and more in-depth information about the animal world. Presentations at the Wild Wonders Outdoor Theater are designed to encourage active and healthy living and engagement with the natural world in a fun and stimulating format.

Five

The Forest, Hard Times, and a Fort

The regal green glory of Point Defiance Park has always been most apparent in the reaches beyond the bustle of its gardens, waterfront, and zoo. The park's forested region, which still commands the majority acreage of the peninsula, has by design experienced far less development since the City of Tacoma first received permission in 1888 to craft a park out of the rugged wilderness. As early as 1902, the Board of Park Commissioners held the position that stewardship of the old growth forest was a paramount mission of park administration. Five Mile Drive, a misnomer of actual linear distance, leads to the peninsula's outer point and, though rough, was already largely in place by the time the Hare & Hare Plan of 1911 advocated its embellishment with multiple picnic grounds. For the most part, however, the forested region of Point Defiance remained far less traveled at a time when most visitors arrived by boat or streetcar for their day in the developed areas of the park.

After the introduction of limited road and picnic amenities to this region of the park in the early 20th century, the decade of the 1930s brought significant changes to the forested areas. During the Great Depression, work crews funded by federal relief agencies such as the Civilian Conservation Corps (CCC) and the Works Progress Administration (WPA) spent thousands of man-hours building the first road down to Owen Beach, improving trails, clearing brush, building a water culvert system, constructing community kitchen picnic shelters, and dismantling the dilapidated 1892 Rustic Bridge, which they replaced with 23,000 cubic yards of earthen fill and a new roadbed. Perhaps the most significant project of this era, accomplished by citizen volunteers aided by the CCC and WPA, was the reconstruction of Fort Nisqually on a Point Defiance Park bluff overlooking the waters of the Tacoma Narrows. It had originally stood some 15 miles farther down the Sound.

Even before the city of Tacoma gained municipal title to Point Defiance Park in 1905, park board secretary M.L. Clifford wrote with prescience in 1902, "many thousands of people from all parts of the United States visit this park and are there enabled to see the native timber of Puget Sound in its native state. The timber in this great country is rapidly being cut down along the lines of travel, and in a very few years it will be necessary to go long distances away from the established lines of travel to see this timber in its natural growth. It becomes a matter of interest to all the people of the United States to preserve in some place easy access to some tract of land covered with this natural growth."

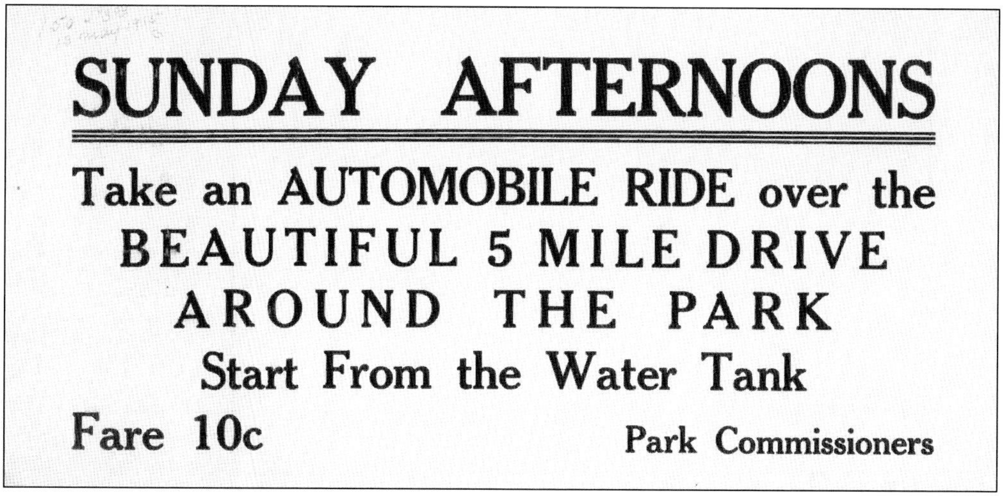

At the turn of the 20th century, the vast majority of Point Defiance Park visitors arrived by water or on the streetcar. In the early days of limited private car ownership, primitive road conditions kept many visitors from venturing into the park's forested reaches. In 1915, the park board implemented a shuttle service that ran at regular intervals from the Water Tank (see page 42), around Five Mile Drive, and back. Some 5,000 visitors patronized the service that first season, more than covering the board's cost of providing it. Below, an early private automobile emerges (against today's one-way traffic flow) from the entrance to Five Mile Drive; the posted speed limit is 15 miles per hour. The hand-hewn railings of the 1892 Rustic Bridge are visible just beyond the log-posted gate.

Since exploring Point Defiance Park was so much more of a truly pedestrian experience in the first two decades of the 20th century, myriad footpaths, walks, and byways traversed the wooded slopes. The title of this postcard indicates that the locale was one of the routes to reach the 1903 waterfront pavilion.

This view of another path through the woods must have been in proximity to the previous one, as the windows and the lower boat storage piers of the octagon-shaped 1903 waterfront pavilion are just visible through the tree branches at center left. The pavilion was surrounded by a wooden deck, to which many paths and rustic bridges led.

The paths through the woods included tree specimens felled either intentionally or perhaps naturally during the previous storm season. The visitors shown here found one such future nurse log to be a handy perch during their stroll. Their attire would seem to preclude a more vigorous word for their outing, such as *hike*.

The Point Defiance Park system of intersecting wooden paths did not consist merely of dirt trails. Where the terrain dictated, staircases of hewn logs aided in navigating the changing elevations, and boardwalks bridged gullies and small ravines on the way up and down the bluffs. Most of these features are long gone from the park.

Some of the routes through the forests of Point Defiance Park were suitable for either pedestrian or early automobile travel, provided that the unpaved driveways were passable in the climate of Puget Sound, of course. The above photograph records the prospect for visitors who departed the main road near the Lodge and followed the curving driveway down to the 1903 waterfront pavilion; the same curve in the now-paved road still exists today. The left image, from the summer of 1907, details another means for pedestrians to navigate Point Defiance Park's steep slopes—one requiring agility, fearlessness, and, preferably, trousers.

During the Great Depression, crews funded by federal relief agencies such as the CCC and the WPA were at work in the forests of Point Defiance Park. Camp Point Defiance, housing some 200 CCC workers, stood on the bluff just below the present-day site of Fort Nisqually. This view over the rooftops looks down the Narrows toward the site of the future Narrows Bridge.

The young men of CCC Company 935 at Camp Point Defiance join in song in their barracks after a day of brush clearing and trail building. The camp opened in the autumn of 1934 and served as a winter camp. CCC members were between the ages of 18 and 25 and made $30 per month, $25 of which was sent home to their families. (Courtesy TPL.)

A view of the mess hall at Camp Point Defiance shows the relatively finished appearance of the accommodations. If not exactly luxurious, it was dry. The term *winter camp* meant that the CCC crews were not housed in tents, as they would have been in a summer-only camp such as those established at higher elevations in the mountains. (Courtesy TPL.)

One of the nicknames for the CCC was "Roosevelt's Tree Army," referring to the president's creation of the corps to provide meaningful work-relief projects in the forests across America. One of the young men working in CCC Company 935 at Camp Point Defiance, Elbert Cranfill, vividly recalled the odor of mothballs from the surplus World War I uniforms they wore while working. (Courtesy TPL.)

The WPA also figured prominently in the work accomplished in the forests of Point Defiance Park in the 1930s. The WPA crews were generally older than the young men of the CCC, and they worked on rotation in many of Tacoma's parks as well as on other public works projects across the city. These photographs show specific projects in Point Defiance in the winter and spring of 1936. The WPA worked on drainage construction for the pond in the park's entrance area (above). WPA crews also rebuilt a log pedestrian bridge leading from the Pagoda (which was by then the Point Defiance Park bus station) to the main picnic area (below). The WPA bridge was itself replaced in the late 1950s when a major traffic revision leading away from the waterfront necessitated its relocation. (Courtesy WSHS.)

One of the most visible WPA projects in Point Defiance Park was the construction of community kitchen picnic shelters, such as the one next to Fort Nisqually. These popular gathering spots of the past 70 years have hosted countless picnics and family reunions, protected visitors from sun and rain, and provided the added convenience of running water and a wood-fueled stove. (Courtesy WSHS.)

Another WPA task in the forests of the park was the production of cedar roofing shakes and shingles, not only for the picnic shelters, but for many wood structures in Point Defiance and other Tacoma parks; two workers pose here with an impressive stack, perhaps in the area near the present zoo, which housed a small sawmill and lumber operation.

These small concrete and river rock culverts can be found on Five Mile Drive, part of another WPA project to help channel water drainage away from the drive through the Point Defiance forest. In this example, small white pebbles spell out "WPA" and the date "1936."

While unknown WPA workers spelled out their own markers in the culvert system, there are a few more formal markers placed throughout Point Defiance Park. Citing the year that the WPA spent working alongside community groups and historical societies on the restoration and reconstruction of Fort Nisqually, this stone marker has stood adjacent to the site for some 70 years.

The work that both the CCC and the WPA accomplished for the restoration and reconstruction of Fort Nisqually was acknowledged in these photographs from the late 1930s. Above, the men of CCC Company 3224 posed formally in November 1937 in front of the Fort Nisqually bastion and palisade with their supervisors, who hailed from the ranks of the Army, the National Park Service, and the US Forest Service. In the more casual grouping below, one of the crews of the WPA takes a break in February 1936, posing adjacent to the front bastion of Fort Nisqually to present a gold watch to the crew's foreman, William Pitcher. (Courtesy TPL.)

The sales shop, front palisade, and bastion of Fort Nisqually are essentially complete in this photograph from September 1, 1934. The work underway in the foreground is the squaring and shaping of additional pickets for the remaining three sides of the palisade that surrounded the reconstructed historic site; Fort Nisqually's original site was 15 miles south, near DuPont.

Another photograph from September 1, 1934, taken just inside the front gate, shows additional workers with adz and ax, squaring beams for the Fort Nisqually buildings with post-in-sill construction. The project sponsor, the Young Men's Business Club, planned a large public dedication that Labor Day weekend for the completion of the restoration's first phase. (Courtesy TPL.)

In the summer of 1934, the Young Men's Business Club apparently decided that bathing suits and heels were the perfect workplace attire for the forests of Point Defiance Park, and, incidentally, as publicity for their Fort Nisqually project. Frankie Cowan (right) poses with an unidentified lady lumberjack. (Courtesy TPL.)

This c. 1936 photograph, looking through the front gateway of Fort Nisqually, shows the restored Factor's House, one of two original fort buildings moved from DuPont. The Young Men's Business Club and the WPA by this time had completed the surrounding sides of the palisade, as well as the rear bastion. (Courtesy TPL.)

The reconstruction and restoration of Fort Nisqually was considered complete at last on June 9, 1940, when the Young Men's Business Club and the Metropolitan Park District marked the occasion with festivities dedicating Fort Nisqually as a "Pioneer Museum." This aerial view shows the locale around 1937, judging by the postcard caption, though a few structures were still to be added before 1940.

This view of the front of Fort Nisqually shows how wide open the area was in 1940; a few fir trees have been planted in the rough grassy area in front of the palisade. Through the main gate, the farthest building visible is a small house built for the various resident caretakers of the next 40 years.

The Factor's House was one of the original buildings relocated from the original DuPont site. "Factor" was an administrative title of the Hudson's Bay Company, which had built the original post in the 1830s. From 1940 to 1980, the structure housed assorted curios, but was not an accurate representation of the house's history. The couple on the porch is believed to be Frank and Alida Gloyd, the first resident caretakers.

Between 1980 and 2002, the Factor's House contained a small museum focused on Hudson's Bay Company history. After a major restoration based on extensive research, the Factor's House was rededicated as a historic house museum in 2003. As part of the educational programs for today's park visitors, volunteers Mike Froslie (left, at top of steps) and Lyle Hegsted portray historical figures who lived and worked at Fort Nisqually in the 1850s.

While the 1930s restoration of Fort Nisqually saved two historic structures and reconstructed a number of others, the historical accuracy of the site from 1940 to 1980 was open to opinion. Two views of the Factor's House parlor from the same angle, taken 60 years apart, illustrate the difference. In the c. 1945 photograph above, an unrelated grouping of artifacts does not offer the park visitor an engaging experience; many of the items would not have been in a Hudson's Bay Company fort of that time and place. The below photograph, from around 2008, records the parlor's restored historical setting. The volunteers are, from left to right, Nancy Keller-Scholz, Linda Myers, Lissa Wilson, Pam Wilson, Nancy Rowan, Ruth Cannon, and Cassie Young. They are ready to offer park visitors a lively interpretation of Fort Nisqually's past, based on study of the historical record. Note the photographer's image in the mirror!

One of the defining features of Fort Nisqually Living History Museum's presence in Point Defiance Park since 1980 has been the emphasis on scholarship and the historical record of the Hudson's Bay Company's 19th-century presence in the Pacific Northwest. Over the past 30 years, Fort Nisqually has also become a destination for professional excellence in regional history education. Above, special events coordinator Peggy Barchi introduces one of the site's heritage chickens to a delighted father and daughter, Jeremy and Kylee Doty. At left, volunteer Bryan Browne (left) and site supervisor Mike McGuire bring in the Yule log for the special public celebration of a 19th-century Christmas. Such occasions add to the signature public educational experiences available throughout Point Defiance Park.

Along Five Mile Drive, between the Vashon Island and Dalco Passage Viewpoints, stands The Mountaineers Tree. With increasing appreciation of the heritage of the old growth forest in this region of Point Defiance Park, the park board, in cooperation with the Mountaineers Club, first marked this 450-year-old Douglas fir with a plaque and an interpretive sign in 1949. Rededicated with a new sign in 1989, The Mountaineers Tree emphasizes appreciation for the preservation of the park's old growth native forest in the middle of today's urban metropolis. At right, park visitors Jessica Trujillo and Ryan Little lend a sense of scale to the tree. In the photograph below, park staff members (from left to right) Stan Carter, Matt Shierven, and Chris Little install the latest version of the sign in 2012 in conjunction with the club's centennial.

By the late 1930s, the CCC's Camp Point Defiance faced a significant reduction in its workforce as the national program was curtailed. After it was no longer required by the CCC, the site of the camp was made available for the park's summer recreation purposes. Although the buildings were eventually removed, the area was used for many years thereafter as Madrona Day Camp, introducing generations of Tacoma children to the pleasures of having a forest close to home. In this photograph from June 27, 1939, Girl Scouts roast hot dogs over an open fire during their day camp week at the former CCC Camp Point Defiance. Shown here are, from left to right, Lucy McIntyre, Laydel Green, Juanita Clark, Phyllis Elsworth, Ruth Strom, and Dorothy Allen. (Courtesy TPL.)

Six

Something for Everyone

From picnics to concerts, from train rides to horseback riding, from children's nursery rhymes to salmon bakes, Point Defiance Park's over 700 acres have always contained something for everyone to enjoy. With its close proximity to the city, visitors from near and far have been drawn to the park's beauty, with its formal gardens, old growth forest, waterfront, and a variety of attractions.

As Bernice Newell, reporter for the *Tacoma Daily Ledger*, wrote in 1903, "[parks] are all the resort the great army of busy people have." Indeed, Point Defiance has served as a resort for generations of people wanting to enjoy the park's natural beauty and popularity. Countless personal and family memories have been made over the years as people gathered to celebrate special occasions, enjoy a refreshing break from their daily routine, or partake in the fun of a special event or attraction.

In addition to the public amenities throughout the park, private enterprises have partnered with Metro Parks Tacoma over the years to offer even more options for people visiting Point Defiance. While some park activities like picnics and open-air concerts have been popular pastimes from the park's earliest days, other attractions and amenities did not stand the test of time for one reason or another. Nonetheless, they are all an integral part of the Point Defiance story.

In 1909, the Alaska-Yukon-Pacific Exposition, or World's Fair, drew thousands of people to Seattle, but there were still many who chose the simpler pleasures of Tacoma's Point Defiance Park. This group of unidentified picnic-goers found that Point Defiance made a delightful stop in the summer of 1909. Even when out on a beachfront picnic, the group's attire includes jackets, ties, hats, and gloves. The photograph above shows their arrival in the park, perhaps using the wheelbarrow in the foreground to help transport the heavy picnic basket. The photograph below finds them comfortably situated on the beach, where a close examination of the spread on the tablecloth reveals sandwiches, deviled eggs, and a large can of pork and beans. The gentlemen of the party evidently took turns taking these photographs.

Large groups have flocked to Point Defiance's popular picnic grounds for decades. The main picnic area, located on a plateau above the beach with wonderful views of Puget Sound and Vashon Island, has been a feature of the park since the early 1900s. The photograph above indicates the popularity of this locale. Additional picnic shelters in the park's forest region were described around 1915 as having fireplaces with 3-foot-by-6-foot concrete stoves and stone chimneys. The photograph below shows a close-up of the cooking stove in the above picture, where a woman wearing a hat with a large white feather manages several pots and kettles. There is also a large can of Cottolene on the stove top. Cottolene was a brand of shortening made of beef tallow and cottonseed oil used as an alternative to lard.

On July 8, 1899, the Tacoma Military Band provided musical entertainment for members of the National Editorial Association and their wives during a clambake at Point Defiance Park. The Military Band was directed by Julius Adler and played daily concerts in Tacoma parks, traveling from site to site on a tiny private streetcar. (Courtesy TPL.)

Concerts have long been a popular form of entertainment at Point Defiance Park. The entry bowl of the park forms a natural amphitheater for large gatherings to enjoy music. The second annual United Service Organization (USO) Music Festival was held on July 28, 1946. It was attended by over 7,000 people. One of the featured performers was the 70-piece Youth Symphony Orchestra of the Pacific Northwest. (Courtesy TPL.)

On May 30, 1933, an amusement park called Funland opened in the park. Located to the right, or east, of the park's main entry road, Funland was a private enterprise that met a need for family entertainment during the Great Depression. A percentage of its profits was paid to Metro Parks Tacoma, thus providing much-needed revenue for the park system.

The Board of Park Commissioners was concerned that all the entertainments provided at Funland be safe and appropriate for families. They insisted upon trying each one of the rides before the park opened to the public. Rides included The Dodgem, Merry Mixup, Buzzer, Tilt-a-Wheel, and the exciting Water Scooter, shown here.

Funland gave visitors to Point Defiance Park an escape from the hard times and worries of the Great Depression and World War II. Longtime residents of the neighborhood can still remember the mechanical sounds of the rides and the shrieks of laughter emanating from the park on warm summer evenings. However, by 1965, Funland was no longer profitable, so the owners removed all the rides and attractions except the Cart Track. Throughout the 1970s, various organizations proposed redeveloping the Funland area, but all were declined by the park board as being incompatible with the park's natural environment.

Shortly after the zoo's buffalo exhibit closed in 1930, the old buffalo barn was put to use as the home of the Point Defiance Riding Academy. The academy was founded in 1933. Privately owned horses could be stabled on-site, or academy horses could be rented to enjoy the more than 12 miles of bridle trails that crisscrossed Point Defiance.

Charles F.T. (Chen) Rowe is seen here running toward the camera with Sanka, one of the horses that boarded at the Point Defiance Riding Academy. The academy was destroyed by a fire on August 20, 1964. When the other horses were too frightened to flee the fire, Sanka leapt forward and broke through a Dutch door to safety. Following Sanka's lead, 12 other horses also escaped, and Sanka was proclaimed a hero. (Courtesy TPL.)

Salmon bakes have been a tradition in the Northwest for generations. At Owen Beach in 1962, a popular summer salmon bake tradition started that lasted over 20 years. Initially, the salmon bakes were held on a weekly basis as a complementary event linking Tacoma with the larger regional events surrounding Seattle's 1962 World's Fair. In successive years, the salmon bakes were held several times each summer and frequently featured fireworks displays and Native American–themed events. Above, tickets are for sale from women wearing pearls with their paper headdresses for the occasion. An adult dinner cost only $1.50. Below, the crowds are obviously enjoying the delicious food and their decorative headgear.

The Camp 6 Logging Museum opened in 1964. Owned and operated by Western Forest Industries, the museum was a recreation of a logging camp from the early 20th century, when "Loggers were Boss and Steam was King!" Exhibits included camp cars from Quinault, bunkhouses from Kapowsin, a variety of steam donkeys, and a Shay steam locomotive whose whistle could be heard throughout the park as it traveled along the tracks through the woods. A special attraction each December, the Santa Train, delighted children of all ages as the festively decorated train took a 20-minute ride around one and one-fourth miles of track. Financial considerations forced the museum to close in 2011, and the collection was sold to a train museum in California.

Opening on July 4, 1964, Never Never Land was a privately owned concession within the park. The attraction showcased nursery rhymes and storybook themes, where the young and young-at-heart could walk through beautiful wooded trails as they went from scene to scene populated with fiberglass figures. Although initially very successful, the attraction closed in 2001, a victim of rising costs, vandalism, and reduced visitation. Above, Isabelle Havel is seen leading two young visitors through the entry of stacked books. Below, one of the most popular exhibits in Never Never Land was the giant shoe of the "Old Woman Who Lived in a Shoe" nursery rhyme. Children could climb a flight of stairs abutting the brightly painted shoe and enjoy the thrill of riding down a slide inside.

Here a young man patiently awaits 1:00 at the Hickory Dickory Dock exhibit to see the mouse that had run up the clock run back down at the appointed time. A furry toy mouse made this trip numerous times per day. Other storybook themes included Little Boy Blue, Jack and Jill, and Old Mother Hubbard.

Young Anne Litwin, the small girl in the foreground, visited Never Never Land in 1967 with, from left to right, Steve Litwin, Dave Litwin, Briggs Bott, Sharon Litwin, Julia Bott, and Karen Fengler Nicholas, who is holding Patty Litwin. In the background, Goldilocks can be seen running away from one of the Three Bears. (Courtesy Anne Winters.)

On June 9, 1973, the first Sound to Narrows run was held, when 305 hearty souls braved the eight-mile course. Starting at the Point Defiance Boathouse, the course wound through the hills of Five Mile Drive and finished at Vassault Park. In the days before computer timing chips, each of the finishers received a tongue depressor with their finish place recorded on it. This Tacoma running tradition grew by leaps and bounds. In 1979, divisions were added for wheelchair participants and military units. To this day, the military units continue the tradition of running in uniforms and boots. Due to the growing crowds, now numbering over 10,000 people, the racecourse changed several times over the years before settling on the 12k course that starts and ends at Vassault Park but still travels the park's scenic Five Mile Drive.

Often-remembered features of Point Defiance Park are the large wooden slider swings that dotted the landscape from the 1920s through the 1960s. This simple attraction was guaranteed to elicit a smile from all who rode them. A trip to the park became so much more fun when you stopped to enjoy a swing during your visit. Right, Sheree Hiller and her brother Gary enjoy a ride on the swings in 1959. Below, James Frederickson and his sons, Timothy, age two, and James, age four, visit the swings in the late 1940s. (Right, courtesy Sheree Trefry. Below, courtesy Jim Frederickson.)

Even though all who visit Point Defiance Park know that it is a uniquely beautiful place, in 2011 the American Planning Association made it official by naming Point Defiance one of the Great Places in America. Seen from the air, Point Defiance's forested peninsula stands as a canopied sentinel to the city of Tacoma, with Mount Rainier in the distance. In turn, citizens have taken to heart Hare & Hare's 1911 admonition that "every citizen of Tacoma should feel it a duty and privilege to become one of the guardians" of the park. As Metro Parks Tacoma works to maintain the park for more than two million visitors each year, the importance of planning for the future is not lost on those wanting to assure that the park remains "Tacoma's Great Pride."

Image Credits

The authors are grateful to all who allowed use of their photographs to bring the history of Point Defiance Park to life. All photographs not credited are part of the collection of the Metropolitan Park District of Tacoma. Photographs from the Washington State Historical Society are credited as WSHS, and those from the University of Washington are credited as UW. The photographs of the Tacoma Public Library's Northwest Room are identified below:

Cover	Boland B104407
Page 13	TPL 1001
Page 20	Arthur French DC-059
Page 34	Boland B7358
Page 41	TPL 9693
Page 48	Image #7435
Page 49	Boland 18478
Page 59	G14.1, #029
Page 62	Boland B22416
Page 63	Richards D31389-4
Page 69	Richards A858
Page 71	Boland B10413
Page 72	Richards D8583-16, Richards D9937-8
Page 73	Boland B16633, Richards D9937-33
Page 74	Richards D34477-4, Richards D17702-6
Page 83	Boland B17647
Page 84	Richards D755-2
Page 99	870-7
Page 100	870-5, 870-2
Page 104	TPL #6908, T76-1
Page 105	804-10
Page 106	G74.1 #129, E16-2
Page 116	General Collection LOY-001, General Collection HBS-012
Page 119	Richards D12024-1